Pebble® Plus

Exploring Space

Space Vehicles

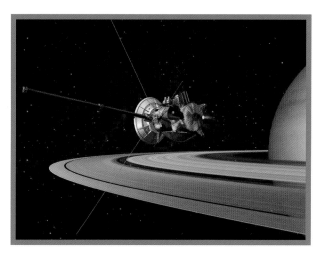

by Martha E. H. Rustad

Consulting Editor: Gail Saunders-Smith, PhD

Consultant: Ilia Iankov Roussev, PhD
Associate Astronomer & Associate Professor
Institute for Astronomy, University of Hawaii at Manoa

CAPSTONE PRESS
a capstone imprint

Pebble Plus is published by Capstone Press,
1710 Roe Crest Drive, North Mankato, Minnesota 56003.
www.capstonepub.com

Books published by Capstone Press are manufactured with paper
containing at least 10 percent post-consumer waste.

Library of Congress Cataloging-in-Publication Data
Rustad, Martha E. H. (Martha Elizabeth Hillman), 1975–
  Space vehicles / by Martha E. H. Rustad.
    p. cm.—(Pebble plus. Exploring space)
  Includes bibliographical references and index.
  Summary: "Full-color photographs and simple text describe space vehicles and the work they perform"—Provided by
publisher.
  ISBN 978-1-4296-7580-2 (library binding)
  ISBN 978-1-4296-7896-4 (paperback)
  1. Space vehicles—Juvenile literature. I. Title. II. Series.
  TL795.R87 2012
  629.4—dc23   2011027950

Editorial Credits
Erika L. Shores, editor; Alison Thiele, designer; Kathy McColley, production specialist

Photo Credits
Getty Images/AFP/Alexander Nemenov, 19
NASA, 5, 15, 17, Jerry Cannon, Robert Murray, 7, JPL, cover, 1, 9, 13, 21
NASA/JPL-Caltech/R. Hurt (SSC), 11

Artistic Effects
Shutterstock: glossygirl21, Primož Cigler, SmallAtomWorks

Note to Parents and Teachers

The Exploring Space series supports national science standards related to earth science. This
book describes and illustrates space vehicles. The images support early readers in understanding
the text. The repetition of words and phrases helps early readers learn new words. This book
also introduces early readers to subject-specific vocabulary words, which are defined in the
Glossary section. Early readers may need assistance to read some words and to use the Table of
Contents, Glossary, Read More, Internet Sites, and Index sections of the book.

Printed in the United States of America in North Mankato, Minnesota.
102011   006405CGS12

Table of Contents

What Are Space Vehicles?

Space vehicles travel far from Earth. Probes, satellites, rovers, space stations, and other spacecraft are used to learn about space.

Soyuz spacecraft at the *International Space Station*

Powerful rockets launch vehicles into space. Some rockets fall off when the fuel is used up. Other rockets help vehicles move around in space.

No Passengers Allowed

Probes fly deep into outer space.

Some tell scientists about

other planets or moons.

Other missions look at comets

and asteroids.

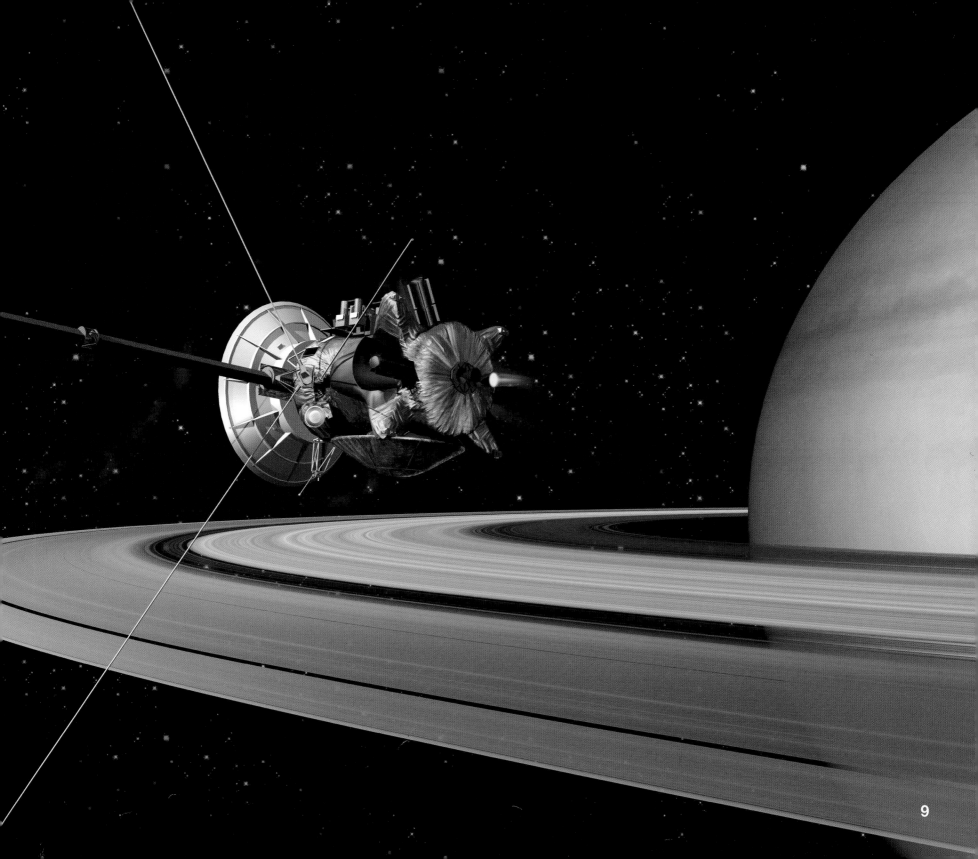

Satellites travel around a planet, moon, or star. Computers on board gather information. Radios send that information back to scientists on Earth.

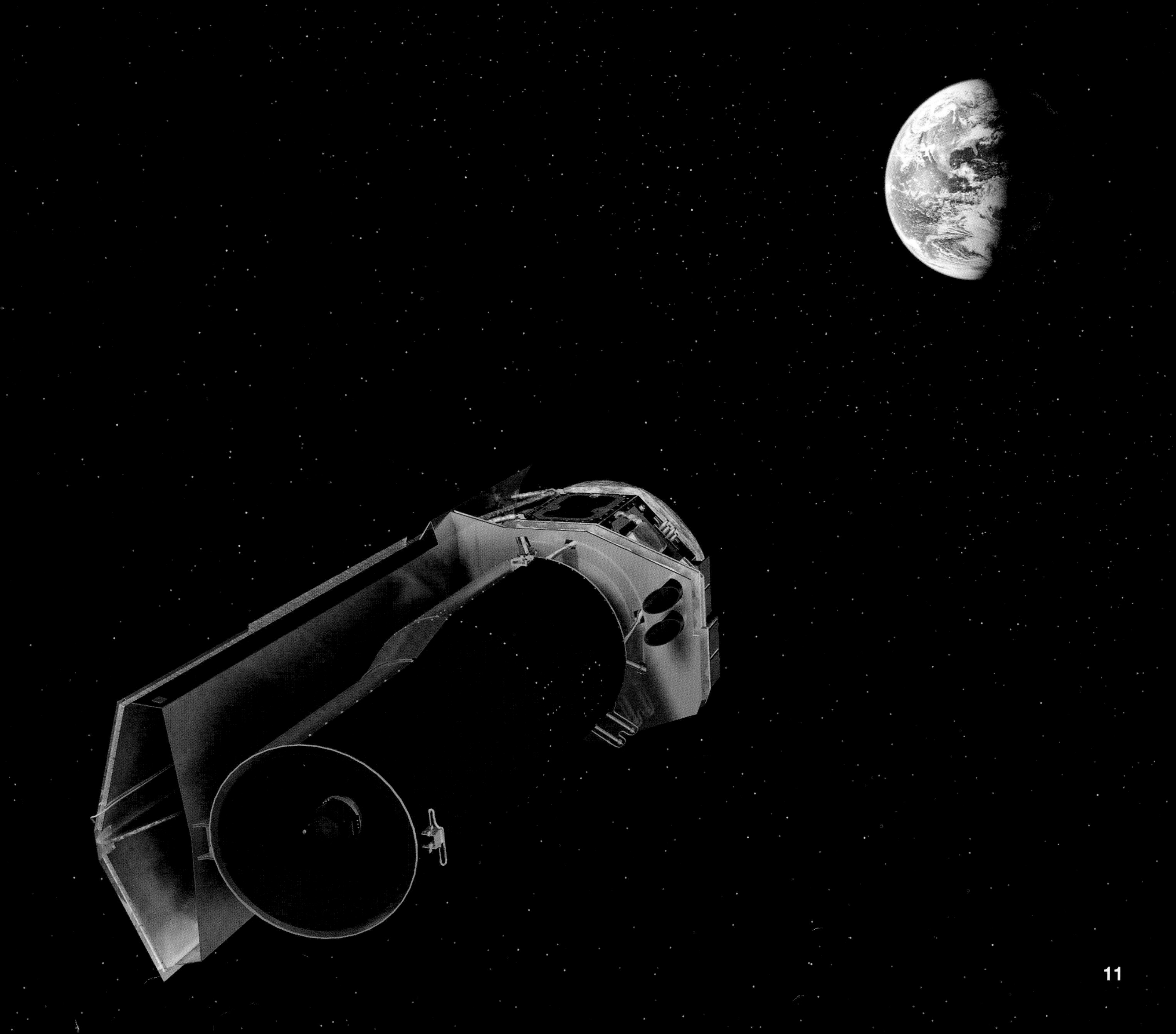

Rovers travel on other planets.

These robots take pictures

and study rocks.

Scientists on Earth send signals

to tell rovers where to go.

Astronauts on Board

For 30 years, space shuttles
carried U.S. astronauts
to and from space.
The last shuttle flight was
in 2011.

A space station orbits Earth.

Astronauts live on board.

The *International Space Station* was built in space. Sections were launched from Earth.

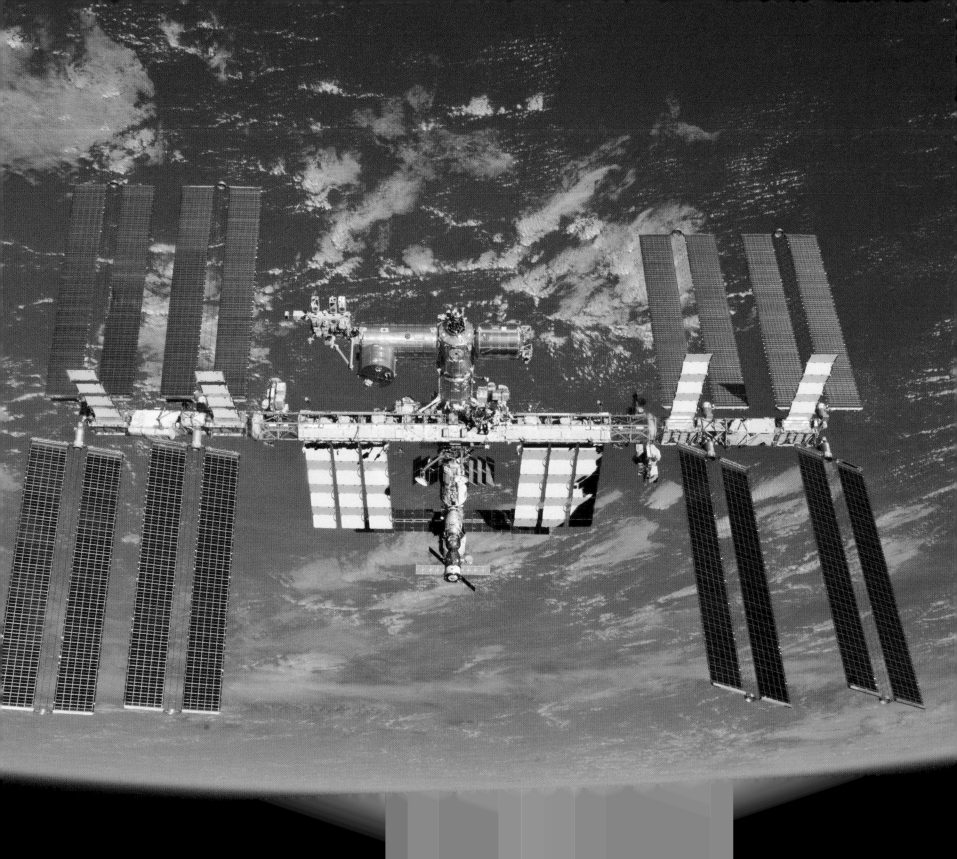

Russia's *Soyuz* spacecraft travels into space. The *Soyuz* takes Russian and U.S. astronauts to and from the *International Space Station*.

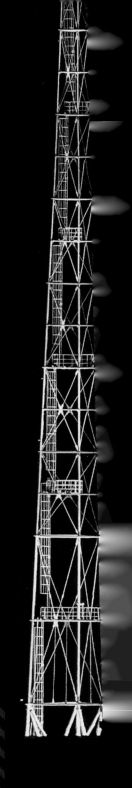

The Future of Space Vehicles

Scientists plan future missions.
Probes and rovers will tell more
about other planets and galaxies.
Someday space vehicles may
carry astronauts to other planets.

Glossary

asteroid—a large space rock that moves around the Sun

galaxy—a large group of billions of stars, planets, dust, and gas

mission—a planned job or task

orbit—to travel around an object in space

probe—a small vehicle used to explore objects in outer space

rocket—a long, tube-shaped object that moves by pushing fuel from one end

rover—a small vehicle that people can move by using remote control

satellite—a spacecraft that circles Earth or another object in space

space shuttle—a U.S. vehicle that carried astronauts into space and back to Earth

space station—a spacecraft that circles Earth in which astronauts can live for long periods of time

Read More

Conrad, David. *Exploring Space.* Earth and Space Science. Mankato, Minn.: Capstone Press, 2012.

Gross, Miriam. *All about Satellites.* Blast Off! New York: PowerKids Press, 2009.

Tagliaferro, Linda. *Who Walks in Space?: Working in Space.* Wild Work. Chicago: Raintree, 2011.

Internet Sites

FactHound offers a safe, fun way to find Internet sites related to this book. All of the sites on FactHound have been researched by our staff.

Here's all you do:

Visit *www.facthound.com*

Type in this code: 9781429675802

Super-cool stuff! Check out projects, games and lots more at **www.capstonekids.com**

Index

Word Count: 195
Grade: 1
Early-Intervention Level: 22